IN THE LIFE,

THE TRAPS *and the* *Freedom*

IN THE LIFE,

THE TRAPS *and the* Freedom

SHAUNA ROCK

iUniverse, Inc.
Bloomington

IN the LIFE, The Traps and the Freedom

iUniverse books may be ordered through booksellers or by contacting:

iUniverse
1663 Liberty Drive
Bloomington, IN 47403
www.iuniverse.com
1-800-Authors (1-800-288-4677)

ISBN: 978-1-4759-1102-2 (sc)
ISBN: 978-1-4759-1103-9 (ebk)

Printed in the United States of America

iUniverse rev. date: 04/03/2012

CONTENTS

ACKNOWLEDGEMENTS

I want to First thank God who is my Rock and Anchor. To my Pastor Isaac Hicks and, First Lady Hicks of True Word Life. To Pastor Bond of The Citadel of Worship and Praise, a Special thanks to you. Pastor Bond thanks for advising me that I have a story to tell and for laboring in prayer for me. I want to thank those who were instrumental in my life. I want to thank Missionary Brenda Harris who prayed for me. I want to thank my friend Raynard Smith who prayed for me and encouraged me to write this book. I want to thank Juanita Bynum, my mentor, through all her preaching's and her deliverance book, ***No More Sheets.*** To Joe Dallas, author of **Desires in Conflict.** Thanks Apostle Kim Brewer author of ***Take a Step Up.*** Thanks Apostle Brewer for encouraging me to write. To Liberty Savard, author of ***Breaking the Power of unmet needs,***

<u>unhealed hurts, and unresolved issues in your life!</u> Thank you family and friends. A Special thanks to my dear Sis, Desiree Peterson who inspired me many years ago to write a book while looking back at her . . . Eyes wide open with a blank stare! Well here I am!!

DEDICATION

First and Foremost I want All the Glory to go to God from this book. This Book is also dedicated to my late father, Ernest Robinson who has always inspired me to be the best. Thanks dad for your wonderful words of encouragement.

About Author

Shauna Rock is a native of Brooklyn, New York and the older of two children.

Upon establishing a spiritual life, I accepted Jesus Christ at a young age in my teens. I have always felt like a calling was on my life but didn't know what it was. I had a feeling. I have served in church on different auxiliaries and continue to serve. I am under my Pastor Hicks at True Word Life Ministry. This book is an autobiography of my life. I discuss my formative years of life into adulthood. The many challenges, choices, and triumphs that I have faced. The good thing of it all is learning that I can always get up again. There is a ladder to your success and I found out who that ladder was; it was God. God was and has been there every step of the way. He is the very reason why I live today and was not consumed.

My Formative Years

*(Jeremiah 1:5) "Before I formed thee in the belly
I knew thee; and before thou camest forth out of
the womb I sanctified thee, and I ordained thee a
prophet unto the nations."*

I lay before you in your hands; In the Life. Well my childhood was special and I think a little different from some children. I came from a broken home with one parent, my mother. My father was an absentee parent. My mother separated me from my father and his family because of his addiction. My father was an alcoholic and she didn't want me being raised or around him. While my mother was getting her education, into her profession she sent me to live with my grandmother, my mother's mother in Trinidad.

As a child, I didn't understand this. I felt like my mother abandoned me and there was a hole in my heart. The bonding was broken and the nurture v. nature stage was interrupted. When I mean interrupted, there wasn't any bonding or that touch to make you feel loved. At that stage, you feel it before you can actually comprehend what it is. This is considered the development stages.

My mom did what she had to do to survive, as she knew how. By no means, do I blame her for this. The rejection was a seed that was planted inside of me and as I grew into an adult, so did it. See the devil, the adversary knows about your life. He knows what buttons to push to cause a reaction in you. A child feels rejected when their parents are not around. For me at this time, both were not around. I was in a different country and my father was in New York. This was the way I felt and my feelings were valid. As a child you don't know about life and how it works. You just know the parents that you look up to or suppose to look up to, are not around.

My grandmother did a marvelous job. She instilled God in me and took me to church. She nurtured me and she made education a priority. She was not my parents, nor was it her responsibility to raise me. My grandmother sent me back to New York after really missing my mother. She thought it was time, but the trust was never restored. As I got older, I realized that. The bonding process was interrupted and there was a breach. Now I am back in East New York, Brooklyn with my mother.

My mother is a native from Trinidad and my father, a native of New York. My moms' rules of discipline were extremely different from my father's family. I just want to pause right here and let you know, I have loved my mother and still do love my mother. I just want to inform you of different cultures and beliefs. Being raised by a West Indian mother to me was very difficult because, my mother was to the extreme of discipline. Definitely different from what I observed of my friends parents. My mother believed in harsh discipline. She believed in beatings which I received. This deepened the hurt in our relationship. Discipline was to prevent me from going astray but this was abuse. Well to my mom's dismay, it didn't prevent me from going astray. I think it was my boost; I went on to do my own thing headstrong. I know things were not easy for my mother by any means; she worked hard. I saw her struggle to make it in her career as a registered nurse and as a single parent. This frustration that she was experiencing at that time of her life was definitely transferred to me. My grandmother has and is always been the apple of my eye.

If you are anything like me, grandparents come with this extra special grace from God. Grandmas' bake cookies, nurture you, and stand in the gap with God. While my mother worked 16 hr shifts my heart longed for her because, I missed her and needed her. I was a latch key kid at age six years old. A latch key kid for those who are not familiar with the term is, a child who has a key to get in their home.

An unbelievable young age and, I was so scared because, there was no one home to greet me. Sometimes, I would have a family member or a babysitter to watch me. It just was not the same. I felt abandoned and did express this to my mother. The pressure was on her to have her career. Nothing changed and I felt terrible inside. Lonely, rejected and without parents. As a child, this is how things are perceived in their mind. **(Isaiah 49:15)**" *Can a woman forget her suckling child, that she should not have compassion on the son of her womb"? Yea, they may forget, yet will I not forget thee.* God says in the passage a mother can forget her child but he will never forget us. He will comfort us and heal our hurts. I had a gaping hole for love and nurturing inside. I had the finer things in life and lived in a gated community, nice clothing, and food and went to Catholic School. I felt so detached and no Love from my mother and didn't know where my father was.

I didn't know my father's family and where they were. My mother kept that information from me until I was 13 yrs of age. My grandmother had convinced her that it was time for me to meet my father and father's family. My mother was angry about this because she did not want me to know any of them. The way she explained it to me was: she didn't want me exposed to my father's alcoholism and his family. She said they were a lot of drama and kept mess going on. I was very sure that I wanted to meet them and be a part of that family because I was already a part of them anyhow.

They were my family regardless of what kind of drama was going on. I met my aunt Linda first and then Aunt Salome and then Aunt Nancy. My mother and I was going through the motions of life but living a dysfunctional life at home. I think my mother not having a man around to share the responsibility of raising me was First of all; my mother was at work most of the time. As I got older my responsibilities increased. I had to clean, cook and take care of my sister. Eventually, I went on to high school. I really wasn't allowed to go out and enjoy my life as a teenager. My mother didn't allow it. She was strict and I basically was to go to school, do chores and be home. When I didn't comply, my mother beat me which left marks on my body. When my mother use to beat me and I use this terminology because, this is what it was to me; I felt anger and hate.

It was something more to these beatings. This wasn't a child that needed discipline because the punishment didn't fit the crime at all.I felt like my mother was trying to kill me. One time that I remember vividly after one of the beatings, my mother kept me home from school. She didn't want anyone in school to find out. I never told anybody,

I kept it in. I use to fight a lot as I was growing up with other children, my peers. Well as I went on to high school, I went to a hookie party.

For those who don't know what a hookie party is, it is when you don't go to school and go to a party instead. I went because I wanted to be with my friends. So I went to this hookie party and got raped. While at this party the music was playing and we were having a great time. Then all of a sudden, guns were pulled out and I was raped at gun point. I didn't tell my mother but I remembered looking up at the sky and seeing that my whole world looking differently. I was scared to tell my mom and then a couple of days later a friend's mother came with me to tell my mom. My mother never comforted me, no hugs and no kisses. My mother was very distant toward me. My mother just kept making me feel like it was my fault. She kept saying that she sent me to school and not a party. She was right about the not sending me to party but, I did not deserved to be raped. I was been scolded at a time that I should have been comforted. Those undertones made me feel like it was my fault. The police was notified and brought in and, they took me to the hospital.

They had apprehended the rapist and I had to identify him. That was terrible because, he could see me. He was in a bubble cell and to me he was looking right inside of me. I felt like I was being raped all over again. His piercing eyes were demeaning and I was terrified. While at the hospital, they took a rape kit and gave me the routine shots to prevent STD's. The time of the rape, I was age 14 and a ***virgin . . .*** I didn't understand why I was bleeding and in pain.

Physically and emotionally, I was a mess. The psychological trauma was unbearable. The pain was too much for me to bear. All that time something was preserving me, God. For such a traumatic thing to have taken place, I was still able to function but in a daze. I went outside and looked in the sky and immediately the sky looked differently. It had a cloud in it and I couldn't understand why me! I still did chores at home because that's what was expected of me. In that particular era, parents were responsible for the decisions of prosecution of the perpetrator. My mother decided not to prosecute; this was a sad day for me. I wasn't happy about this decision not to prosecute. My mothers' reason not to prosecute my rapist was because she was protecting me from being badgered on the witness stand.

Maybe there was some validity to that. So many victims are told it's their fault. Thank God today no matter how old the victim is; she has the choice of saying yes or no. Even in some cases today, the State takes over and the victim has no say. I'm very happy about this, very. While going through this emotional state, I was so confused. So now I'm back to school and my rapist walks right by me. With a blank face and, no feelings. It was a cold, long walk and I was so scared.

He had shown no remorse through it all. In an instant I was very angry that he was allowed to be free and victimize again. I was very surprised that the school allowed him to come back. Then it dawned on me, he was never convicted. After all he was released and not charged with a crime. I was very angry at my mother that she would make me go back to the same school. I was scared and embarrassed. How could I act like everything was ok? That is what my mother expected and I couldn't even phantom her reasoning.

In our house it was kick the dirt under the rug and back to life as usual. I was 14yrs old, a virgin and I was raped by some Thug, just that I was raped by gunpoint. I was raped and had to go on like everything was fine in my life. As a child, my mother said whatever goes on in this house, stays in this house. She also told me that children were to be seen and not heard. She learned that from my grandmother.

It was very hard to go to my mother and tell her that someone took advantaged of me. I was scared of being punished. We didn't have a platform like that. Our relationship wasn't normal as a mother and daughter should have been. We had a very dysfunctional relationship. There was never closeness and I always distrusted her because of what occurred in my earlier years. We never discussed sex; it wasn't a free topic in our household. I learned about sex in the street and from friends.

A discussion of sex seemed to be Taboo in my mom's house. Eventually, I was transferred to another school because of the rape. It was real traumatizing going to that school. It was like I was reliving it daily and the worst part, school was a cloud. From that moment of being raped and returning to school, any school, I was not interested in anything. Things completely changed for me. My mother and I relationship became more estranged as ever. I never thought it could get any worse but, it did. We were living in the same house but were not conversing at all. I had a hole even deeper inside of me than I can ever really imagine. I couldn't put a finger on it and didn't know why I felt so empty inside. The emptiness was screaming, help, help. Please somebody help me. There was no relief. I always knew there was a higher being but didn't know what or who. I was young and didn't know at all.

Well the estranged relationship between my mother and I stirred up my curiosity about my father and his family. Later on down the line I would go to my father and stay with him in Arizona for three months. I told my mother that I wanted to go and see him. So she packed me up and at age 14 I went to see my father for the first time that I can remember. As my mother packed my bags and got me ready for the flight to visit him, she was very angry.

I don't know how she was feeling inside but, she said a lot of hurtful things to me. She stated you want to see your father and I have protected you from him all this time. My mother told me that my father is a drunk. There were a lot of negative remarks about my father that I had to endure. I never heard anything positive about him at all. We all know that relationships don't start out negative. I asked my mother if there was anything positive about my father, she replied don't ask her, her business. After the rape, I made a decision to visit my father.

My mother was very reluctant and my grandmother convinced her to send me. She was very angry and stated "Don't come back until you are 18 yrs of age." I asked my mom was she serious and she said yes. Don't come back until you are 18. I only wanted to visit and not live with him. I wanted to find out who my father was inspite of his drinking. Well, I arrived in Phoenix, Arizona where he was residing at that time. I met him for the first time and it was awkward. I never told him about the rape because I didn't feel comfortable.

Back then, I bottled everything up inside. My father was drunk everyday for the 3 months that I visited. He had a wife, who had 4 children. I couldn't believe what was going on. He was with some woman who had 4 children and he only had 1 biological child and that would be me. On one hand I couldn't understand why my father wanted to be with this woman and help her with her children. On the other hand; I thought because, of his alcoholism my mother didn't want to be with him.

He needed to be with somebody, I guess! I always felt that my father chose being an alcoholic over having me as his daughter. I reunited with him at age 14 but years were lost. Time is not a thing that you can ever expect to recapture. Well, one day he was arrested for disorderly conduct and that was when his wife found an opportunity to send me back to New York. I wouldn't be going home because my mother didn't want me back remember until age 18. I would go home to my aunt, my fathers' sister. My father died on May 15, 2010 from medical conditions. He never dealt with his issues and chose to become an alcoholic. Before he died, he encouraged me a lot and I wanted to take care of him while he was sick. He refused because of his dignity. I did get him a Case Manager for someone to look after him. He didn't like that because he was very independent.

He needed that structure because he wasn't consistent in taking his medication and eating a proper diet. Call it pride or dignity, he wouldn't let me. The kind words that he said to me meant a lot. He was my biological father and I needed his affirmation and his approval for my life. Most young ladies look for that approval and love from their father. This is a normal aspect of a young girl's life. It's like the first touch from the womb.

If a lot of kids would get this touch it would change their entire lives. It is the simple things that count and we find unimportant. From birth a child learns from their parents what caring, nurturing, and love is all about. A girl looks to her father to teach her about a man's love. A father protects her and teaches her what to do, put up with, or not. God was so instrumental in setting up the two starting from Adam and Eve. He did great and it was without imperfections. Man was left to follow what God ordained for our life.

THE TRAPS

(Job 18:10) "The snare is laid for him in the

ground and a trap for him in the way."

I was disappointed and vulnerable after trying to get the help from my mother and father. In no way did I receive help from either. My understanding of this is because; they both had their own problems and could no way help me. My mother didn't get the help for me from the rape because it was back to business as usual. My father never knew because he wasn't in any shape to help. He was drunk the entire time that I visited him.

Upon returning to New York with my Aunt who is very dear to me, I looked for outside help to cope with my difficulties in life. I was now 15 yrs old and interested in boys. Remember no one ever discussed sex with me. Therefore, I had no guidance into the decision that I was getting ready to make on my own. I had my first sexual experience with sex at age 15. It was very powerful for me because I gave someone permission to touch me.

It seemed to me that I needed that immediately. It was so soon after the rape and when I gave permission to my boyfriend, I felt that I was back in control of me. This was a very powerful decision for me. This would also be my downfall because I started looking for a boyfriend to fill that spot and to make me whole.

I was young and he was four years older than me. I didn't know anything about statutory rape back then. I was young and vulnerable. To add insult to injury, he was an alcoholic and abusive. Of course he was and that's why he sought out someone as young as I was. I thought I was in love but, was far from it. I experienced domestic violence at age 15.

Even as I got older I had a boyfriend stab me in my hand and cut my back because he didn't want me to end our relationship.

He also tried to stab me in my stomach and the blade broke before our eyes. I saw the confounded confused look on his face. I knew that was God right there. If he would have succeeded, I would have died. Throughout, I had quick fixes, a quick fix for an incomplete me. I had a deep hole inside of me that only God could fix, heal, and put back together again. Like humpty dumpty, God can only put me back together again.

While in my youth, I was supposed to be enjoying my life but I didn't. The choices that I made in my life were based on what I didn't receive as a child. I really didn't know which way to turn except into the arms of someone who loved me or appeared to love me. I really didn't know what that face or heart looked like. I went by my feelings at 15 yrs old and I continued to go on feelings throughout my life. When this relationship was complete and I got out of it; I found out that I was going through cyclic emotions and feelings. I eventually grew up and still managed to keep that hole in my soul, in my heart and kept those memories in my mind. I repressed the rape and acted like it didn't happen. When I went away to college I started being affected by the thoughts and seemed like it started to torment me. I sought out counseling in school but then stopped. I repressed it again and again. I didn't want to deal with it because it was too painful.

I used to think why I should deal with something that I didn't afflict on myself. Think about it, is there anything that you don't want to deal with in your life. The fact is, in our life we must deal with things in our life to go forth. We usually don't and, then that thing deals with us with a vengeance. We need to take control of it before it takes control of us. By me not dealing with this issue completely, created a trap for myself.

This was an area and a tactic that the enemy could use. **(1 Peter 5:8)** *"Be sober, be vigilant; because your adversary the devil, as a roaring lion, walketh about, seeking whom he may devour."* So our enemy, the devil knows enough to torment us or try and stop us. This is why it is important for us to deal with these issues in our lives as they come up because; its festering ground for our common enemy. Although we repress and suppress these issues, they have not gone away. They are just waiting for a moment to interrupt our lives and cause havoc. After the unhealed hurts, unresolved issues, and unmet needs, I still continued to fill those places with boyfriends. When I got tired of boyfriends; I said that I am through with men and wanted a woman. Well I got just what I said. **(Proverbs 18:21)** *"Death and life are in the power of the tongue: and they that love it shall eat the fruit thereof."* (**Matt 12:37**) "For *by thy words thou shalt be justified, and by thy words thou shalt be condemned."*

God doesn't like idle words and we will have to give an account for our idle words. God gave us power through our words. We have the power to make things happen by our speech because in the beginning God formed us in his own image. In the beginning God said let there be and it was. **(Genesis 1:3)** *"And God said, Let there be light: and there was light.* I got a girlfriend because I said I wanted one first.

My belief was a girlfriend would understand me much better and understand my emotional needs. I thought my girlfriend would be there for me and meet my needs and I would meet hers. Nothing could have been much further than the truth, Nothing. That was a TRAP. Yes, a trap. As you continue to read you will soon realize. I honestly thought that another woman would be the one. I think that we all go into relationships expecting the very best and a positive outcome. For me, I really thought that being with a woman was my answer. I tried boyfriends and they did not work because of the abuse and control. One I thought, hey a woman is my answer to happiness. I felt that she would treat me the way I deserved to be treated. This relationship with who I will call Ann, a factitious name of course. Our relationship started out beautiful and we were extremely close. The feeling was unlike no other. I was very open and for the first time I felt very much complete.

This feeling of happiness and completeness was what I lived for everyday. Remember I had a major gap and felt unloved by my mother and never had that traditional Father and daughter relationship either. This was the very first time that anyone touched my inner need of completion. It was finally done and I was never going to let that go. We were inseparable and completed each others sentences. We were never apart and always together. I remember saying that this relationship was worth me going to hell.

I wanted that to last forever because I have never been touched in my inner core. The very soul and my being were in Love which I would later learn was lust. The feelings that I was feeling was just that, feelings. I felt so complete at the time because, I never dealt with the issues from childhood and the rape. Ann and I came together with some similar background and we meshed together. Emotionally we were there and feeding off of one another. We truly needed each other for survival. We did everything together. We spend everyday and all day together listening to music and going out sometimes. Our bond was very tight. The only way that I can describe it to you would be like a drug addict. It was a dependency like a drug addict in dire need for their next fix. That is the only way for me to describe the urgency within me for being with Ann.

I was hooked and did not want to be unhooked. As children we rely on our parents for everything. We rely on them for food, safety, emotional needs, nurture, comfort and most of all protection. This is how women become dependent on one another and form a relationship. Girls and women form these relationships from a natural need that a parent was supposed to give. Since the parent didn't give this during the course of childhood; the child or woman will continue to seek this until it is completed.

The thing about being with a woman, which I was in the Life for about 12 years, it never is completed. The more the dependency, the more you want more and more. You can't get enough love, comfort or nurturing. The hole just gets deeper and deeper. (**Deuteronomy 5:7**) "Thou *shalt have none other gods before me.*" I had put someone before God. She was morning breath and my evening breath. This was like idolatry. God forbids that because, we are not to live without God and not people. The fact is God has placed a place within all of us that no one can fill, ever. We are not supposed to live or breathe someone else. God comes first always even in a traditional relationship. See this is a way for the enemy to twist things in our lives. He knew about my childhood and what was void in my life; then he presented something that would make me feel whole for a moment. God wants us to be whole in every area in our life.

I would have never been whole being a lesbian because; it totally went against God's order. It is against the way God created things from the beginning. You can refer to Genesis to read how God created the earth and mankind. (**Leviticus 18:22**) *"Thou shalt not lie with mankind as with womankind: it is Abomination."* I would see men in the street in passing and they would flirt; I would feel very sick to my stomach and nauseas. I literally felt sick and wanted to throw up.

I wasn't even aware that I felt that way about men until one tried to talk to me. In my mind I wanted to rid men out of my life completely. I mean, I truly hated men. They couldn't flirt with me, speak to me, and God forbid if they touched me. Oh my God, I didn't know how much my soul couldn't bear this. Being in the life, came with restrictions and many changes. By no means was the rejection and alienation easy to handle. Ann made it all worth the while; it was us against the world. I lost friends and family and I didn't care. At that time, I thought that something was very wrong with them. Being in the life is what they call it if you are a lesbian or gay. Being in the life is a separate world out there. There are different rules and regulations. There is a lot of jealousy involved and I also experienced it tremendously. It comes with the lifestyle in almost all of these kinds of relationships. Any and everyone are considered a threat to the relationship. Your security is wrapped up into that one person and can't be shared. It's unhealthy of course. Jealousy never ends well ever.

It's an obsession and there is no amount or affirmation or time that fills that gap inside. Remember a mother is a nurturer and some dads too; if that relationship is broken it can have some devastating effects on that child. It creates abandonment issues, unhealthy relationships form and dependency relationships.

"That's why many women fall into dependent relationships without knowing what's really happening to them. They can go for years without closeness, and then suddenly they meet someone who taps into their deepest longings. It begins innocently enough, appearing to be nothing more than a nice friendship. Gradually, though, the friendship becomes a snare. Both parties become more reliant on the relationship, giving it priority over everything else." Desires in Conflict, author Joe Dallas (p.206). This is exactly how it happened for me and once I found that person who tapped into my deepest longings, I fell deeply.

This particular longing was based on neediness and not being whole. Everything about it felt like love but it wasn't. It became strangling because you really couldn't be independent at all. I remember one time Ann told me that she was all the friend that I needed. When she said that something clicked inside of me but I ignored it. In the interim, everyone else was neglected. She never liked the close relationship that my aunt and I had.

She always felt that it was a threat. Ann also didn't like me speaking with men because she said men and women couldn't be friends. She always said that men only want one thing from a woman. My effort to have my own identity outside of this relationship became a challenge. We became verbally abusive towards one another. I started realizing how unhealthy our relationship had become. Not realizing that it was always unhealthy.

I experienced a lot of verbal and emotional abuse. Eventually, it graduated to cat fights, fists fights. I knew then that it was time for us to go our separate ways. The problem was I couldn't leave. I knew about God and went to church every now and then; I just could not leave. I have just committed myself to a wrong desire and created a soul-tie. A soul tie is the product of wrong agreement between two people.

The following is a prayer to break soul-ties:

"Lord, I have been looking for another human being to fix the need and the pain inside of me. I have not made right choices and kept my relationship with this person in proper perspective. I want to be free from any emotional, intellectual, or self-willed ties I've let form, and I repent for allowing this to happen. Forgive me for having sought satisfaction and fulfillment from anyone other than you. I now loose, cut, and sever any and all soul-ties I have

willingly or ignorantly entered into. I reject these soul-ties and every soulish satisfaction they have provided for me. I loose them; reject them, renouncing them and every wrong agreement I have ever come into that birthed those soul-ties in the first place. I bind myself to the truth of your love, care, faithfulness, mercy, and grace. Your grace is sufficient for all my needs, hurts, and issues. I am choosing to bring my needs and vulnerabilities to you alone. I will no longer let fear overcome me when I feel defenseless and vulnerable. Instead, I will remember that this means I am in a place where my soul's walls and defense systems are down. I choose now to realign my thinking and confess that this is not a bad place to be. It is a good place to meet you-there on top of the fallen defenses and tumbled walls. I will quickly call out to you to come as deep into my soul as you can, touching every dark spot with your grace and mercy. This vulnerability can surely be used as an open door to your grace. God, no matter how quickly my soul might try to reestablish its protective bars over it. I will not hesitate to run through this doorway towards you, for if I am not sure of what finally tumbled the defense systems I've been loosing, then I'm not sure how long they might stay down. There will come a time when they are completely gone, when my soul surrenders totally to you; but for now, I will continue to loose them until they can no longer be reactivated. I've tried too long and too unsuccessfully to get my own soulish, human expectations fulfilled. Increase my awareness of the fallibility of my unsurrendered soul's expectations. Increase my awareness of old patterns of behavior I need to loose. Increase my awareness of the wrong thinking I need to loose and reject. Increase my awareness that I can trust you with everything I let you get close to. Help me to recognize every high thing I've allowed my soul to put up between me and you, and I WILL PULL THEM ALL DOWN. In Jesus' name, Amen. (p.171-172) **Breaking the Power, author Liberty Savard.**

At this point I made a decision that I wanted my desire to change. I had been a lesbian for 12 yrs and my desire changed completely when I gave my life completely to God. I prayed the above prayer to break soul-ties and I went for an alter call for deliverance in church. Most of all, I made a decision in my mind. See it is a decision like choose whom ye shall serve (**Joshua 24:15**) *"Choose you this day whom ye will serve."*

It is as simple as choosing. A relationship with anybody or thing that controls you or abuses you in any way is not of God. God gave us all a choice from the beginning. He is a gentleman and never forces himself on anybody. Therefore, we should never feel forced, controlled, or abused in anyway to stay in a thing. I got delivered from being a lesbian and chose to serve the Lord instead.

The Freedom

(Galatians 5:1)" Stand" fast therefore in the

liberty wherewith Christ hath made us free, and be

not entangled again with the yoke of bondage."

I would like you to pause right here and pray. Ask God to enlighten your spiritual eyes to see what God has placed in your spirit to receive. This by no means was easy. The first manuscript of this book I deleted. I told God no, Im not doing it because everyone will know my personal business. I got sick and, I was going through emotional and spiritual warfare. Spiritual warfare is your spirit wrestling with your soul.

Our soul is where our mind will and emotions are; it is what we call our flesh. Our spirit is what God saves and it's usually compliant with God. So our spirit and soul war against one another. One wants to be saved and the other doesn't. I want to let you know that there is freedom. I went through a lot and found freedom in Jesus. I don't know about you but, I felt weighed down when I was in sin. It's such a weight that you can't explain and it feels extremely heavy.

(Hebrews **12:1**) *"Let us lay aside every weight, and the sin which doth so easily beset us, and let us run with patience the race that is set before us.* The Bible is so clear because it clearly states for us to lay aside every weight and move forward. Although I deleted the first manuscript, it did not change anything. Purpose kept bubbling on the inside of me and I felt like something was missing. I felt like God wasn't pleased with my response and therefore, he wasn't pleased with me. I started from scratch again to carry out my assignment. God will never ask you to do something very easy in your purpose. It will always be something challenging. You won't be alone though; God will be with you every step of the way. Initially, I had asked God what was my purpose in this life.

I wanted to know what I could do to help others. He sure answered me! Be careful what you ask for because you just might get it. Only the Lord knows what has gone on fully in my life. Now you do too for the most part. Know this . . . . You are not alone in your struggles and pitfalls. We are all challenged in that area. The Bible states in (**John 16:33**), *in the world ye shall have tribulation: but be of good cheer; I have overcome the world.* God is letting us know that we have a helper in him.

Jesus is the hope of Glory. If you have struggled in the area of homosexuality or some other area of bondage, there is a way out! Tired? Feel like you are going crazy? There is a way out! Give it to Jesus because he is equipped for the battle! (**1 Peter 5:7**) *"Casting all your care upon him; for* *he careth for you.* You can give your life completely over to God. You can be a son or daughter of our Father.

(**John 3:16**) "For *God so loved the world, that he gave his only begotten son that whosoever believeth in him should not perish but have everlasting life."* You can have everlasting life if only you believe. You can be saved right now where you are if you just say these words. (**Romans 10:9**) *"If you shall confess with your mouth the Lord Jesus and shall believe in your heart that God raised Him from the dead, thou shall be saved."*

You can confess with your mouth now, Father in the Name of Jesus, please forgive me for all of my sins, I repent from all my sins. Come into my heart and save me. I now confess that you are Jesus Christ my Lord and Savior. I believe that you died for my sins and paid the price for me. Thank you Jesus for saving me and giving me the gift of eternal life, in Jesus name, Amen.

If you prayed that prayer, you are brand new creature in Jesus. Get into a local church that teaches the word of God. Keep your spiritual ties for strength. (**Romans 8:1**) *"There is therefore now no condemnation to them which are in Christ Jesus, who walk not after the flesh, but after the Spirit."* This means that your past is your past. You are now a new person in Gods sight and have passed from death to life.

You now have eternal life in Jesus if you walk after the spirit and not the flesh. Congratulations on your new life; you are now part of a royal family.

Scriptures That Helped Me With My Deliverance

(Romans 1:24-32) "Wherefore God

(Genesis 2: 18)

(Genesis 2: 21-24)

Footnotes

1. Quotations by the Kings James Bible.

2. Desires in Conflict, author, Dallas Joe. 1991 Harvest House Publishers.

3. Breaking the Power, author, Savard Liberty. 1997 Bridge-Logos Publishers.

Contact

shauna_rock@yahoo.com

phone number: 347-722-3271